EIGHT RIVERS

First published in 2006
in the United Kingdom
by Charmed Hole Publications
The Bank of Scotland, Main Street
Kyle, Ross-shire IV40 8AB

ISBN 0 9522707 1 4

A CIP catalogue record for this book is
available from the British Library

Printed and bound by Short Run Press Limited, Exeter EX2 7LW

www.atisha.org.uk

To Paul Jeanes,

with best wishes

Atisha Thegregom Auld

25. X. 2013

EIGHT RIVERS

A TRIBUTARY OF WORDS

BY

ATISHA MᶜGREGOR AULD

PUBLISHED BY

CHARMED HOLE
PUBLICATIONS

And he shall be like a tree
Planted by the rivers of water

PSALM 1

I will run
Run the rivers
Till they run dry
I will search
Search for the well of wisdom
And leap at its fount
Till knowledge returns
And drink
Drink again from the waters of time
Then measure Aquarius against the scales of man

If no balance is found
I will drift
Drift away
On the current tide
On the seventh wave
With the wave of a crest
To be seen no more
Save in the mind
So farewell sailor
Salmo salar

I hear the sound of a train

In the stillness of the night

I disappear

Badger's sett
Set up
Exterminate
Tuberculosis
Cattle, calves

Immunise
Ecosystem
Disarray
Black and white
Red tape

We will stand
By a tree
You and me
And the sound
Of our love
Will be drowned
By the song
Of the birds
Rejoicing above
At our passion
In the foliage below

Chinese silken shoes
An everlasting fetish
Bound for tiny feet
Beauty is crippled
And shuffles alone
The route of a lifetime
The silk road

Let the sea not haunt you
Nor the clouds o'erhead
I will cuddle you my little darling
Till the stars have all fled

The moon will awake you
When she smiles from on high
Till then my little darling
I will sing a lullaby

Play in the ocean
Swim in the deep
My little darling
Sleep, sleep, sleep
Sleep, sleep, sleep

C

Let the sea not 'aunt 'ee
Nor the clouds o'er'ed
I 'ull cuddle 'ee me lidl 'ansum
Tull the stars 'ave all fled

The moon 'll awake 'ee
W'en 'er smiles from on 'igh
Tull then me lidl 'ansum
I 'ull sing a lullaby

Play in th' ocean
Swem in the dayp
Me lidl 'ansum
Slayp, slayp, slayp
Slayp, slayp, slayp

Bracken fronds
No longer trampled under hoof
Merlin and twayblade
The lesser be
Camouflaged fritillary wings
Fly up on high
Rhododendron
Brings a temporary burst of colour

Ticks transmute
And commoners dwindle away
Their weakened powers
Leaders are impotent
And know not the great scheme

The past lies in terror
Beneath the long moor grass
Watching predators, machinery and herbicides
Dart at random
Across the remote, wild and tranquil space
Then with Hecate
Sinks deeper into the mire of the unknown world

But who will carry the lit flame
And blaze a trail across the moor?
Which entrusted life form?
Perhaps the wind knows
And in the fullness of time
You will see it unfold
From the highest hill
To the rocky valley

Until then leave piles of pale cakes
Of barley and oats beside cross roads
Where roads cross
And leave Nature to herald her route
Along the new way to the hastening horizon
So the secret may travel
In the unspoilt waters
That rise from the upland moor

Your heart stopped
So did mine

Beating a retreat
Starved of life force
Your veins left you to die
Leaving the leopard to climb
And fight with a strength
You always had

Now the sap has risen again
But for how long dear friend

At mid-winter look back
cleanse yourself of all ill
remember to kiss
under the mistletoe
to show no malintent

Feast with death in remembrance
of wisdom - its attainment

Sacred wells dry up and sleep
until the snows melt

Red berries symbol of life blood
wait for the re-birth of the sun

Five pointed leaves spiral anew
into the next cycle with curled tendrils

Blue-faced hag of winter
protect cradles with white berries
invoke the power of life
bless holly, ivy and mistletoe
ensure Fertility, Prosperity, Peace

The Lord doth revivify my soul
The walls of his house do edify me
The sound of the organ doth penetrate my thoughts
And the stained glass speaks to me also
The altar strains my body and pierces my ego
But the scent of the lilies refresheth me
And remindeth me of a pure heart and the pain of all sacrifice
The waters of the font taketh me back to my beginnings
Yet my soul treasures all that is herein
And touches peace momentarily
My joy is complete

NMH

The Lord doth re ' vivify . my ' soul:
    the ' walls . of his ' house . do ' edify me.

2   The sound of the organ doth ' penetrate . my
    thoughts : and the ' stained . glass ' speaks
    to . me ' also.

3   The altar strains my body and ' pierces . my '
    ego : but the scent of the lilies refresheth me,
    and remindeth me of a pure heart and the '
    pain . of ' all ' sacrifice.

4   The waters of the font taketh me ' back to .
    my be ' ginnings : yet my soul treasures all
    that is herein, and ' tou . ches ' peace .
    momen ' tarily;

5†   My ' joy ' is . com ' plete.

Glory be to the Father, and ' to . the ' Son : and ' to .
    the ' Ho . ly ' Ghost;

As it was in the beginning, is now and ' e . ver '
    shall be : world without ' end. ' A ' men.

† *Denotes that the last quarter of the single chant should be used*

מִן־הַכִּסֵּא שִׁיר קָדוֹשׁ

יְחַיֶּה יהוה נַפְשִׁי מֵחוֹמוֹת בֵּיתוֹ אֲלַמֵּד׃
קוֹל הַנָּבָל יְעֹרֵר לִבִּי וַאֲשׁוֹחֵחַ בְּפִתוּחֵי מִקְדָּשֶׁךָ׃
כְּזֶבַח בְּמִזְבַּחֲךָ אֶאֱסֹר אֹתִי בְּלִבִּי נָגֳעָתָ׃
וְרֵיחַ הַשּׁוֹשַׁנּוֹת נַפְשִׁי יְשׁוֹבֵב
וָאֶחְשְׁבָה עַל־לֵב טָהוֹר זָכַרְתִּי מַכְאוֹב כָּל־טֶבַח׃
וּמֵי הַיָּם הָיוּ־לִי כְּמוֹ מֵימֵי הַבָּטֶן׃
אַךְ יַעֲלֹץ לִבִּי בְּמִשְׁכְּנוֹתֶיךָ בְּחַצְרוֹתֶיךָ מְנוּחַת נָפֶשׁ׃
לְפָנֶיךָ אֶשְׂמַח לְאֹרֶךְ יָמִים׃

A

Exe
Ex terra
Exeter
Issachar
Isca

N

Ash logs stacked neatly
In a stone alcove
Beside a roaring hearth

A small hand reaches
For a split branch
Carefully lays it to rest
On the crimson pyre

Another hundred years
Dissolves into dust
And returns to ash

A sky crayoned in red
With a sea blue border
Sullied by smoky grey footprints
Of agile aeroplanes
Criss-crossing the atmosphere
As they fly like locusts
From pad to port
Carrying passengers
Oblivious of their fate
West, Middle East, Far East
Arctic North and South
All experiences end in a journey
From which we grow old and die
Or are rejuvenated

Whitethorn berries red
Festal *Cratægus* blossom
Enliven the moor

俳句

サンザシや
野に生気そゝぐ
赤白に

Windows
Push shoppers past
Passers-by
Glimpse goods
For sale
Discount
Buy three
Get one free

Each window
Offers
Its own story
Take me
Upgrade
Pay next year
Shop till
You drop

Window dressers
Dummies
Fooled each one
Into thinking
It ends here
Sorry
No refund
Sold out!

Horses stand in the shade
of the grove
dark tails flicking
in unison
in silence
to the sound of flies

Bronze autumn symbols
beckon both
beginning and end
in unison
in silence
mares and foals part

The herd will remember
the insects
their sharpness of sting
in unison
in silence
as winter winds bite

Spring burgeons again
with vital force
life gives birth
in unison
in silence
progenitor equui

Oeuf
Earth
Hens peck
Green grass
Yellow yolks

Heath
Heather
Ponies graze
Rough shoots
Moor *purpure*

Wheat sheaf
Corn maiden
Scythe sighs
Harvest moon
Fruits golden

Leaf
Leaves
Branches bare
Oak-apple
Russet oaks

Partridge
Pheasant
Copper plumes
Antlers mounted
Shots cease

Huntsmen
Habits
No more
Pink coats
Red fox

Pastoral
Pastures new
Countryside
Allied
To hide, renew?

I touch evil
And shrink away
Time hastes me on
To live my day

Flowering palms
Bid me farewell
Their heady scent
Carries me over the Channel
To the sound of paddled waves

Wild purple flowers
Greet me on the island
Platinum rock and verdigris stone
Sandpipers glint on the sea
While skylarks and gulls
Provide music for swift antics

Day-trippers have little time
To absorb the beauties
The island possesses
But run from monument to shore

I wave at the passengers
As they steam away
They wave back
Not knowing me
Yet we spent
The day together

A few puffins remain *in situ*
Continuing their struggle to breed
Under the auger of St Helen
Who juggles the fertility balance here

Royal Doors open
Incense prevails
Lord have mercy
Heaven and Earth are one

Icons lament
Prayers, humility
Lord have mercy
Where pure candles burn

Holy Mystery
Robe of Truth
Lord have mercy
Bless oil, wheat and wine

Venerable crucifix
Midnight vigil
Lord have mercy
Forgive all transgression

Fast complete
Joyous light
Lord have mercy
Thanksgiving and love

Blessed water
Deities anoint
Lord have mercy
Grant life everlasting

Sacred odes sung
Jesus, Mary, Saints
God of Light
All have mercy

Alleluia, Alleluia, Alleluia

N

Through the thicket
He ran and ran
Flattened ears flying
Cheating the wind
Snout fine and sharp
Amber eyes slanted
Distant coverts call
Invisible quarry gone
Forty miles further

Curled on a couch
Fox passions rise
Rutting season starts
Vague yearnings strong
Submissive vixen poses
Savage flame burns
Dog takes she-fox
Now danger threatens
Sleep in the earth

Cunning, fly and curious
Impertinent, omnivorous
Silver white throat
Tail tipped and coveted
Graceful wild creature
Golden chestnut coat
Speck of red dust
Yoi try-try!
Yoi try-try-y-y-y!

Crown of Thorns
Third eye
Decisions made
Moneylenders out
Exploitation, greed
No need

I go to the Cross
Refusal
To stand down
The Commandment
Remains
Unchanged

Love one another
Give without ceasing
Threefold, one tithe
As God is my Father
I am pierced
To the Soul

Fine pieces were moulded
In timeless motion
Under hidden fronds
O'ertowered by church
Language of bells
And chatter of gulls

Fired by earth
Drawn by fire
Creating destruction
In Celtic paradise
A resting place
Transcending all

Great sculptures thrive
Bronze, granite
Marble and wood
Where goldfish glide
In basket of water
So peaceful a haven

Thanks be to St Eia

N

What deprivation I now know
As though in some monastery
Ageing alone unseen
God never was my thing
Prayer never worked for me
Upward, heavenward
My life was centred on
Violence, hate
Vitriolic acts
Nothing to do with love
I was an outcast
Am still an outcast
Now more than ever before
The evil eye and false gods
Are all available here to me
We cannot survive without
The establishment knows that
Bless these four walls
We all drink from the same
Spiritual cup

King of Kings
Divine Right of Kings
King of the Jews
Kings and Queens
Queen of Hearts
Queen of the Night
Royal Proclamation
Prince and Princess
Regal Heir
Royal Standard
Standing in the breeze
Gentle gens
Shaken by the wind
Taken where
I wist not
Salve Regina
Trumpets awake!

N

Crossed keys
Papal seat
Straight roads
Paths meet

St Peter's domain
Sanctified ground
Rock steadfast
Pietous sound

Mixed peoples
Outdoors pray
Give us a Pope
To head our way

Candles lit
Vigil sure
Souls gather
Life evermore

Seven hills
One dome
Cardinals vote
There in Rome

Holy smoke
Black, white
Church remains
Wielding might

Pontiff chosen
Expatriate wins
Politics influence
Confessional sins

WHEN Moon and Earth
Greet at the equinox
A heightened wave
Walks mysteriously
The great waters
To the chorus

>   *TIDE HO*
>   *CHI RO*
>   *KEEL-RO*
>   *HEEL-TOE*

THEN Ocean and river
Merge into one
Invisibly intertwined
Separating breathlessly
From an overwhelming surge
Energised and purified

>   *TIDE HO*
>   *CHI RO*
>   *KEEL-RO*
>   *HEEL-TOE*

TWO Worlds become one
Then part
Expectant
With the next drawing together

N

Black bird sits on a perpendicular stone
erected by man's heightened understanding
of things tangible and intangible

As we walk widdershins around the ethereal henge
the spherical ring invokes us to encircle it
but is forbidden to release its energy

Static figures cower under modern technology
hearing distant voices from another world
speaking in a code indecipherable

Listen rather to the roar of the ritual traffic
and pray that peace will descend again
on this impermeable everlasting site

N

Destiny or fate
Our lives belong to ourselves
Not to each other

Words fail me
Still in the dark
No explanation given
I am heartbroken
I turn my face away
Enough for now
Time to go
No reply necessary
I love you

: - S
SITD
l : - O
(: - . . .
: ^ U
___ !
Ti2GO
NRN
<3 U

The old man was focused
with moist spectacles intent
on the spectacle of his grandchild
a harpist

She in long low-cut dress
he in matching blue shirt
her fingers plucked feverishly
at the strings

He mopped his sympathetic brow
watching and listening in awe
his own flesh and blood
con amore

The banners in the Great Hall
ten hanging proud on high
swayed silently to the air
on the flute

The conductor's baton rose and fell
to the calming influence
of the *andantino*
then a quick silence

The octogenarian lay slumped
breath frail and failing
Mozart continued to play on
in 'C'

N

I am neither man nor woman
Nor feathered nor finned
The waters flow over me
Yet I am dry
I plunge back into the oceans
Where my voice is heard
With the sun and planets
I gaze inside
To be mirrored often
In the depths of the mind
I hover beside breasts
Both waxing and weaning
And control all that happens
While clustering stars
In contrary forms
With salutary phases
Play silently around
Then I seek out all life
Both introvert and extrovert
You worship me lightly
You worship me darkly
With *AVE MARIA*

N

Your garden looks lovely tonight
Each petal fragrant with the thought of you
Every shrub mirrors the tree behind
All wait expectantly the moist morning dew

The moon will rise alone tonight
Bowing heads incline to her gaze
You will absorb her light wantonly
And gain strength from wise lunar rays

The stars shine brightly tonight
Their shapes guide a myriad of lives
Forget the past and all that has gone
Remember in you nature still thrives

Oh most scented of flowers
Forgive this openness of thought
You know in the vacancy of time
The pleasure to me you have brought

Helios appears above the sky
With dawn warmth, mist and rain
Many a fellow has longed ere now
With you to have erotically lain

Crowned with may
At a Feast
Made for frolicking

Erect stones
With magnetic powers
Dance on the moor

The phallic trinity
Spreads her ears
Man becomes manifest

Pink clouds floating
Leave imprinted lips
On a fragile chalice

Roseate sunset
Falls on the cleave
Of Kestor Rock

Fading skies
Upstage the thoughts seen
Disappearing into the ether

The young moon
Leads the evening mass
Through a medieval leaded light

Oh Gallant Snowdrop!
Galanthus
    Standing alone
    In woodland bare
Foreteller of spring

Oh Brave Snowdrop!
    The mediator
    Between two seasons
A delicate *souvenir*
Of reincarnation

Oh Noble Snowdrop!
In medieval manuscripts
    Pressed on
    Ancient leaves
Is your lasting impression

Oh Elegant Snowdrop!
      Bejewelled
      With fine nectar
Whose seed still multiplies
A thousand years on

Oh Pious Snowdrop!
Revered at Candlemas
      Piercing the snow
      With your purity
La perce-neige

Oh Bunch of Snowdrops!
      Lying gracefully
      On an old man's grave
'Fairmaids of February'
Rest in peace

Love one another
Is deviancy
A defilement?
God created man
In his own image
So men and women
Mix freely
And sing in unison
Together
To God's holy name

Voyage
Voyeur
Variance
Venturer
Veer

Vagary
Vagrant
Visitant
Vandal
Varmint

Veil
Vow
Votive
Vigil
Vespers

Voice
Vowel
Virtu
Vocalist
Volume

Vintner
Vintage
Vessel
Vat
Vault

Veracity
Virelay
Verve
Virtual
Verbiage

Long limbs
Dedicatedly
Detail their way
Gracefully
Through the tense air
To the gaze
Of a thousand eyes
The ball is missed
Served, returned, spun
With the applause
Of a tenacious crowd
Black triumphs over white
But not in the impoverished world

Ringed by rising mists
From the moor
Winsford Hill

Caratacus Stone
Chained in time
Winsford Hill

Exmoor ponies
Oaten muzzled
Winsford Hill

Sheep lazing
Old hawthorn
Winsford Hill

Thatched oak
Packhorse bridge
Winsford Hill

Wildlife roam
Chased, chaste
Winsford Hill

Gypsy wagons
Willow pegs
Winsford Hill

Legendary way
Tarr Steps
Winsford Hill

Hawkridge high
Hidden copse
Winsford Hill

Haunted barrow
Bronze kist
Winsford Hill

Cutting turf
Crying the Moor
Winsford Hill

Iron ore
Win, mine
Winsford Hill

Dunkery Beacon
Focal point
Winsford Hill

Cornwall, Wales
Barle and Exe
Winsford Hill

Barlynch monks
Fish and pray
Winsford Hill

A place to reflect
Dream
Winsford Hill

NM

Winsford Hill

♦

Winsford Hill

Words © Atisha McGregor Auld 2006

Music © Colin Rea & Juliet Field 2006

Ringed by ri_sing mists From the Moor Wins_ford

Hill Ca_ra_ta_cus Stone Chained in time Wins_ford Hill

Ex_moor po_nies Oa_ten muzz_led Wins.ford Hill

Sheep la_zing Old haw_thorn Wins_ford Hill

Tha_tched oak Pack_horse

bridge Wins_ford Hill Wild_life roam Cha_sed,

chaste Wins_ford Hill Gyp_sy wa_gons Wil_low pegs

58

Dun____ke____ry

Bea____con Fo__cal point Wins_ford Hill

Corn_____wall, Wales Barle and Exe Wins_ford Hill

Bar__lynch monks Fish and pray

Wins_ford Hill A place to re__flect

Dream Wins__ford Hill (repeat to fade)

© Charmed Hole Publications 2006

AUSCHWITZ TRIPTYCH 2
Written in memory of those who died during the Second World War in
concentration camps.

CROSSROADS 8
Written on reading a report prepared on behalf of The Exmoor Society -
Moorlands at a Crossroads - The State of the Moorlands of Exmoor, 2004.

EX CATHEDRA *or* SACRED SONG 12
Inspired on seeing a stained glass window in Dornoch Cathedral,
Sutherland, which illustrates St John 15:11.
The sung version is pointed in a single chant, in traditional Anglican style.
The Biblical Hebrew translation has been adapted to the Hebrew Bible
culture and to the idioms of the psalms.
(See Addendum - *In Templo - Sacred Song*)

EXETER *or* ExFe 15
ExFe (Exmoor Iron) was a four year study (2001 - 2005) into the archaeology
and iron ore workings on Exmoor by the University of Exeter, in conjunction
with the Exmoor National Park Authority, National Trust and English Heritage.
Isca was the name used by the Greeks and the Romans for Exeter
in early times.

HAIKU 18

The hawthorn tree has been widely used since ancient times for both festival - May Day - and healing purposes; the Latin name for the species found on Exmoor is *Cratægus monogyna*.

HUNTER'S MOON *or* HARVESTING 22

The Hunter's Moon is traditionally the full moon following the Harvest Moon. The Harvest Moon is the full moon which falls closest to the autumnal equinox.

LUNDY 25

Inspired on a visit to Lundy Island in the *PS Waverley* paddle-steamer. The church and the remains of an old Celtic chapel are dedicated to St Helen(a).

METROPOLIS *or* THE SEE 26

Inspired by the Russian Orthodox Liturgy in London, Devon and Somerset.

PIECES OF BRONZE, PIECES OF EIGHT 31

Written on a visit to the garden and home, in St Ives, of the late Dame Barbara Hepworth.
St Eia was a legendary fifth century saint who crossed the sea from Ireland to Cornwall on a leaf.

THE EXMOOR RIDDLE 42

To be read on a Monday. The answer : NOOW ƎHⱢ.

Based on the Exeter Riddle Book - *Codex Exoniensis* - which contains
riddles in Old English written originally in Latin, perhaps in the
eighth century.

The reference to AVE MARIA may also be construed to read AVE MEA REA.
(See Lewis Stuart's Latin Dictionary)

THOUGHTS ON 'TINNERS RABBITS' 44

Written on a visit to Chagford, Devon and inspired by the
'Tinners Rabbits' (or three hares) found carved on a boss in the local
church and elsewhere in the area. The symbol survives in China on
the Silk Route and in other parts of the world. Each 'rabbit' appears
to have two ears yet there are only three ears depicted in the roundel.

TO A SNOWDROP 46

Inspired on a walk through the North Hawkwell Wood in the
Avill Valley ('Snowdrop Valley') near Dunster, Somerset.

WINSFORD HILL 52

Composed whilst on Winsford Hill, Exmoor in Somerset.
The root of the place name 'Winsford' has been taken from
'**win**' - obtain (ore) from a mine.

IN TEMPLO - *Sacred Song*

The LORD doth revive my soul:
By the walls of his house I am taught.
The sound of the harp awakens my heart,
And I meditate on the sculptures of thy sanctuary.
I am constrained like a sacrifice on thy altar,
Thou hast struck me in my heart.
But the scent of the lilies restores me to life,
Then I think upon a pure heart,
I remember the pain of all sacrificial slaughter:
The waters of the laver have become to me as the waters of
the womb.
Yet my heart exults in thy precincts,
In thy courts there is rest for my soul:
In thy presence I will rejoice without ceasing.

N	end notes
A	addendum
C	Cornish vernacular version
H	Hebrew translation
J	Japanese translation
M	musical version available
T	text message version

WITH GRATEFUL THANKS TO

Editor Kenneth Urquhart
Typesetter Nathan A Dale

ILLUSTRATIONS
Clapper Bridge on Dartmoor John L Hoar
Mr 'Belstone' Fox Leila C Winslade

TRANSLATIONS
Cornish Marlene Hughes
Hebrew Dr Donald F Murray
Japanese Sonoko Strong

MUSIC
Pointing of Sacred Song (Ex Cathedra) Rachel A J Bennett
Composition for Winsford Hill © Colin Rea & Juliet Field

CREDITS
Text message phrases taken from *WAN2TLK? ltle bk of txt msgs*
published by Michael O'Mara Books 2000

Quotation (Epilogue) from *If* by Ted Hughes (Collected Poems 2003)
reproduced by kind permission of his Estate

Photograph of Author Norma McCormack
Reprographics Scriveners, Devon TQ9 5XT
Book designed by Suzanne Snell at Scriveners, Totnes, Devon

"If the sky is infected
The river has to drink it

If the earth has a disease which could be fatal
The river has to drink it"

Ted Hughes

POET LAUREATE 1984-98